ACCOUNTING LIFEPAC
ADJUSTING & CLOSING E

CONTENTS

Author: **Daniel L. Ritzman, B.S.**

Editors: Alan Christopherson, M.S.

    Jennifer L. Davis, B.S.

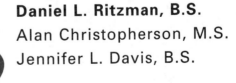

Alpha Omega Publications®

804 N. 2nd Ave. E., Rock Rapids, IA 51246-1759

ACCOUNTING LIFEPAC 7
ADJUSTING & CLOSING ENTRIES
OVERVIEW

The sixth step in the accounting cycle is recording and posting the adjusting and closing entries. After adjusting entries are completed on the worksheet, they must be journalized and posted to the general ledger. The entries made on a worksheet are not entered into the general ledger without first recording them in a general journal.

The **closing entries** are prepared at the end of a **fiscal period** to transfer the balances of revenue and expense accounts to the **Income Summary** account and then to the proprietor's Capital account. This process is necessary in order to close any temporary accounts for an accounting cycle before another one begins.

The **post-closing trial balance** is the seventh step in the accounting cycle. The post-closing trial balance checks the equality of the debits and credits in the general ledger accounts that remain open after the closing process has been completed.

OBJECTIVES

When you have completed this LIFEPAC® you will be able to:

1. Define accounting terms related to adjusting and closing entries.

2. Explain why a worksheet is prepared.

3. Explain why adjustments are made to various accounts.

4. Record adjusting entries from the adjustments section of the worksheet to the general journal.

5. Post the adjusting entries to the general ledger accounts.

6. Explain why closing entries are made.

7. Record the closing entries from the income statement section of the worksheet to the general journal.

8. Post the closing entries to the general ledger.

9. Prepare a post-closing trial balance.

VOCABULARY

Adjusting Entries – entries made in the journal to adjust the ledger accounts so that they will contain the same balances as shown on the worksheet.

Adjustment – an amount that is added to or subtracted from an account balance to bring the balance up to date.

Assets/Expense Adjustment – a type of deferral adjustment that distributes the expense of consumed assets (such as supplies) over more than one fiscal period.

Balance Sheet – a financial statement that reports assets, liabilities and owner's equity on a specific date.

Closing Entries – journal entries prepared at the end of a fiscal period to transfer the balances of revenue and expense accounts to the proprietor's Capital account.

Consistent Reporting – the same accounting concepts are applied the same way for each accounting period for as long as the business operates.

Deferral Adjustments – adjustments to accounts that delay the recognition of the expenses or revenue until a fiscal period later than the one during which the cash was paid or the liability incurred.

Fiscal Period – the length of the accounting cycle for which a business summarizes and reports financial information.

Income Statement – a financial statement that reports the revenue and expenses for a fiscal period.

Income Summary Account – a temporary account whose balance is transferred to the permanent Capital account at the end of each accounting period.

Matching Expenses with Revenue – all revenue and expenses associated with a business activity are to be recorded in the same accounting period.

Net Income – the difference between total revenue and total expenses when total revenue is greater than total expenses.

Net Loss – the difference between total revenue and total expenses when total expenses are greater than total revenue.

Permanent Accounts – accounts that accumulate financial information from one fiscal period to another; also known as real accounts.

Post-Closing Trial Balance – a trial balance completed to check the equality of the debits and credits in the general ledger accounts that remain open after the closing process has been completed.

Temporary Accounts – accounts that accumulate financial information until it is transferred to the owner's Capital account; also known as nominal accounts.

Trial Balance – a proof of the equality of debits and credits in a general ledger.

Working Papers – informal papers in the form of memoranda, analysis papers, and informal reports.

Worksheet – a columnar accounting form used to summarize the general ledger information needed to prepare financial statements.

SECTION I. ADJUSTING ENTRIES

The Purpose of a Worksheet

In LIFEPAC 5 you learned that the accountant uses various methods of providing the owners and managers with the information they need to make good business decisions. The accountant organizes the data that is presented on the formal financial reports by first preparing a **worksheet**. A worksheet is a columnar accounting form used to summarize the general ledger information needed to prepare the financial statements. This important **working paper** analyzes, sorts and updates the ledger account balances for the accountant or bookkeeper. It also provides a single source of information for the financial reports prepared at the end of the fiscal period.

The worksheet helps the accountant to do the following:

1. Prepare the unadjusted trial balance to prove the equality of the debit and credit balances taken from the ledger;
2. Show the effects of the **adjustments** on the account balances to bring them up to date;
3. Sort the account balances into columns according to whether that account is used in preparing an **income statement** or a **balance sheet**; and
4. Calculate the amount of the **net income** or **net loss** for the fiscal period.

The eight-column worksheet organizes the financial information into four sections:

1. The *trial balance section* proves the equality of the debits and credits in the ledger. This section of the worksheet is used to create the formal trial balance which you have already studied in LIFEPAC 4.

2. The *adjustments section* is used to update the balances of accounts such as Supplies and Prepaid Insurance. The balances of these accounts at the end of the fiscal period do not accurately reflect the changes that have occurred due to the daily internal operations of the business. Supplies that were purchased at the beginning of the fiscal period are not used up until a future fiscal period. Since insurance is usually paid for a year in advance, the unexpired insurance must be carried over as an asset for the next accounting cycle. The costs incurred in the operation of a business are expenses, and adjustments must be made to transfer these costs to the proper expense account.

3. The *income statement section* contains the updated balances of all revenue and expense accounts and is used to calculate net income or net loss.

4. The *balance sheet section* contains the permanent accounts of the business and provides all the necessary information to prepare the formal balance sheet and the formal income statement.

The major function of the worksheet as an accounting tool is to show the effects of the adjustments on general ledger accounts. The ledger accounts must be adjusted to contain the same balances shown on the worksheet.

The Need for Adjustments

It is a common practice for many businesses to pay cash for expenses in one fiscal period, but the expense is not actually incurred until a later fiscal period. For example, supplies purchased in large quantities are usually less expensive. Therefore, businesses purchase supplies based not only on usage but also on the cost per item. These purchases must also be divided over various fiscal periods. The Supplies Expense account reflects the actual amount of supplies consumed during the fiscal period.

Insurance policies provide a larger discount if purchased for three or five years instead of yearly. During a monthly fiscal period, the unexpired insurance must be carried over as an asset for the next accounting cycle. The expired insurance becomes an expense for this fiscal period. The Insurance Expense account reflects the actual amount of insurance "consumed" during the fiscal period.

It is important that a business match the expenses with the revenue it produced during the fiscal period. The accounting concept of **matching expenses with revenue**, discussed previously in LIFEPAC 6, states that all revenue and expenses associated with a business activity are to be recorded in the same accounting period. By matching revenue with expenses, a more accurate indication of business performance is obtained than by comparing cash receipts and cash payments for the same period.

These normal business procedures require that accounts be adjusted. The updated balances will provide a more accurate financial picture of the entity at the end of a fiscal period. Adjustments are needed to provide an accurate reporting of the financial progress of the business and its financial position.

The adjusting entries that were considered in LIFEPAC 5 are referred to as deferral adjusting entries. A **deferral adjustment** defers or delays the recognition of expenses or revenue until a fiscal period later than the one during which the cash was paid or the liability was incurred. A major subdivision of deferral adjusting entries is the assets/expense adjustments. **Assets/expense adjustments** are required to distribute expenses over more than one fiscal period. The amounts in the assets account have been posted there for the current accounting cycle or for a prior fiscal period. The adjustment made must determine the portion of the cost that is an expense at the end of the fiscal period. This cost is determined from the company's inventory of office or store supplies used in the day-to-day business operations.

Using the inventory method, it is possible to record each item as an expense when it is removed from inventory. However, this is not a practical method of bookkeeping or accounting. Instead, inventories are kept and the adjustments are made at the end of each fiscal period. These adjustments are made in the adjustments columns of the worksheet.

Journalizing Adjusting Entries

The end-of-period adjustments are computed on the worksheet to provide correct account balances for the financial statements. The accounts in the general ledger, however, still show the incorrect balances. It is necessary, therefore, to journalize the adjustments in the general journal and post the entries to the ledger. After journalizing and posting the adjustments, the accounts in the general ledger will agree with the amounts on the financial statements. The information for the adjusting entries is found in the adjustments column of the worksheet. NOTE: The entries are *not* recorded on the same page as previous entries for the fiscal period but are recorded on the next blank journal page.

The first two **adjusting entries** to be recorded are:

1. An adjusting entry to update the Supplies account, and
2. An adjusting entry to update the Prepaid Insurance account.

Adjusting Entry for Supplies. The information needed to journalize the adjusting entry for Supplies is illustrated on the partial worksheet provided below.

ACCOUNT NAME	ADJUSTMENTS	
	DEBIT	CREDIT
Supplies		4 (a) 1300 00
Prepaid Insurance		(b) 300 00
John's Garage		
Wick Supplies		
Don Donaldson, Capital		
Don Donaldson, Drawing		
Sales		
Advertising Expense		
Insurance Expense	(b) 300 00	
Miscellaneous Expense		
Rent Expense		
Supplies Expense	3 (a) 1300 00	

	JOURNAL				General Debit		General Credit	
Date 20—	Account Title and Explanation	Doc No.	Post. Ref.					
2	1 Adjusting Entries							
May 31	Supplies Expense			3	1300	00		
	Supplies						4 1300	00

Page 2

To journalize the adjusting entry for Supplies, turn to the next blank page of the journal following the last transaction of the fiscal period.

1. Enter the heading *Adjusting Entries* in the middle of the Account Title column of the journal. Using this heading eliminates the need of a source document to verify the transaction.

2. Enter the year and the date in the Date column of the journal. This date represents the end of the fiscal period.

3. Locate the *(a) debit* entry on the worksheet for Supplies Expense and enter the account name and the amount in the Debit column of the journal. Remember when journalizing that the debit entry is recorded first, followed by the credit entry.

4. Locate the *(a) credit* entry on the worksheet for Supplies and enter the account name and the amount in the Credit column of the journal.

Adjusting Entry for Prepaid Insurance. The information needed to journalize the next adjusting entry—Prepaid Insurance—is shown below.

ACCOUNT NAME	ADJUSTMENTS	
	DEBIT	CREDIT
Supplies		(a) 1300 00
Prepaid Insurance		6 (b) 300 00
John's Garage		
Wick Supplies		
Don Donaldson, Capital		
Don Donaldson, Drawing		
Sales		
Advertising Expense		
Insurance Expense	5 (b) 300 00	
Miscellaneous Expense		
Rent Expense		
Supplies Expense	(a) 1300 00	

JOURNAL — Page 2

Date 20—	Account Title and Explanation	Doc No.	Post. Ref.	General Debit		General Credit	
	Adjusting Entries						
May 31	Supplies Expense			1300	00		
	Supplies					1300	00
31	Insurance Expense		5	300	00		
	Prepaid Insurance					6 300	00

The next adjusting entry is for Prepaid Insurance. This journal entry is made directly underneath the adjusting entry for Supplies.

5. Locate the *(b) debit* entry on the worksheet for Insurance Expense and enter the account name and the amount to be debited in the journal. Remember that in journalizing the debit entry is recorded first, followed by the credit entry.

6. Locate the *(b) credit* entry on the worksheet for Prepaid Insurance and enter the account name and the amount to be credited in the journal.

Posting Adjusting Entries

Once the adjusting entries for Supplies and Prepaid Insurance have been journalized, they will need to be posted in order to bring the ledger accounts up to date.

Posting the Adjustment for Supplies. The illustrations below take you step by step through the procedure to post the adjustments from the journal to the Supplies and Supplies Expense ledger accounts.

Date 20—	Account Title and Explanation	Doc No.	Post. Ref.	General Debit		General Credit	
	Adjusting Entries						
May 31	Supplies Expense	4	550	1300	00		
	Supplies	7	120			1300	00
31	Insurance Expense			300	00		
	Prepaid Insurance					300	00

JOURNAL — Page 2

Account Title: Supplies — **Account No.** 120

Date 20—	Explanation	Post. Ref.	Debit		Credit		Balance Debit		Balance Credit
May 1		✔					2282	00	
14		J1	1198	00			3480	00	
31	5	J2			6 1300	00	2180	00	

Account Title: Supplies Expense — **Account No.** 550

Date 20—	Explanation	Post. Ref.	Debit		Credit		Balance Debit		Balance Credit
May 31	1	J2	2 1300	00			3 1300	00	

1. Enter the date in the date column of the Supplies Expense ledger account and the journal page (J2) in the Post. Ref. column.
2. Carry the amount from the journal's Debit column to the Debit column of the Supplies Expense account and compute the new account balance.
3. Bring the balance forward into the Debit Balance column.
4. Enter the Supplies Expense account number in the journal's Post. Ref. column.
5. To post the credit to Supplies, enter the date in the date column of the ledger account and the journal page number in the Post. Ref. Column.
6. Carry the amount from the journal's Credit column to the Credit column of the Supplies account, compute the new account balance and enter it in the Balance Debit column.
7. Enter the Supplies account number in the journal's Post. Ref. column.

Posting the Adjustment for Prepaid Insurance. The illustrations below take you step by step through the procedure to post the adjustments from the journal to the Prepaid Insurance and Insurance Expense ledger accounts.

Date 20—		Account Title and Explanation	Doc No.	Post. Ref.	General Debit		General Credit	
		JOURNAL					Page 2	
		Adjusting Entries						
May	31	Supplies Expense		550	1300	00		
		Supplies		120			1300	00
	31	Insurance Expense	11	520	300	00		
		Prepaid Insurance	14	130			300	00

Account Title: *Prepaid Insurance*   **Account No.** 130

Date 20—		Explanation	Post. Ref.	Debit		Credit		Balance Debit		Balance Credit	
May	1		✔					1200	00		
	31	12	J2			13 300	00	900	00		

Account Title: *Insurance Expense*   **Account No.** 520

Date 20—		Explanation	Post. Ref.	Debit		Credit		Balance Debit		Balance Credit	
May	31	8	J2	9 300	00			10 300	00		

8. Enter the date in the date column of the Insurance Expense ledger account and the journal page (J2) in the Post. Ref. column.

9. Carry the amount from the journal's Debit column to the Debit column of the Insurance Expense account and compute the new account balance.

10. Bring the balance forward into the Debit Balance column.

11. Enter the Insurance Expense account number in the journal's Post. Ref. column.

12. To post the credit to Prepaid Insurance, enter the date in the date column of the ledger account and the journal page number in the Post. Ref. Column.

13. Carry the amount from the journal's Credit column to the Credit column of the Prepaid Insurance account, compute the new account balance and enter it in the Balance Debit column.

14. Enter the Prepaid Insurance account number in the journal's Post. Ref. column.

As a proof that the adjusting entries in the general journal have been posted correctly to the appropriate accounts in the general ledger, the new balances in the Supplies Expense and Insurance Expense accounts will agree with the balances that appear on the income statement. The Prepaid Insurance and Supplies ledger account balances will also agree with the amounts that appear on the balance sheet.

Complete the following activity.

1.1 Use the information on the worksheet below to journalize and post the adjusting entries for **Lawson's Lawn Care**. After completing the exercise, compare the adjusted balances on the income statement and balance sheet columns of the worksheet with your ledger account balances to verify that your work is correct. NOTE: The ledger accounts on the next page are arranged in numerical order.

Lawson's Lawn Care
Worksheet
For the Month Ended July 31, 20—

ACCOUNT TITLE	TRIAL BALANCE DEBIT	TRIAL BALANCE CREDIT	ADJUSTMENTS DEBIT	ADJUSTMENTS CREDIT	INCOME STATEMENT DEBIT	INCOME STATEMENT CREDIT	BALANCE SHEET DEBIT	BALANCE SHEET CREDIT
Cash	7822 00						7822 00	
Petty Cash	300 00						300 00	
Supplies	4319 00			(a)1341 00			2978 00	
Prepaid Insurance	1600 00			(b) 330 00			1270 00	
John's Garage		1630 00						1630 00
Wick Supplies		300 00						300 00
D. Lawson, Capital		9000 00						9000 00
D. Lawson, Drawing	500 00						500 00	
Sales		4367 00				4367 00		
Advertising Expense	86 00				86 00			
Insurance Expense			(b) 330 00		330 00			
Miscellaneous Expense	95 00				95 00			
Rent Expense	450 00				450 00			
Supplies Expense			(a)1341 00		1341 00			
Utilities Expense	125 00				125 00			
Totals	15297 00	15297 00	1671 00	1671 00	2427 00	4367 00	12870 00	10930 00
Net Income					1940 00			1940 00
					4367 00	4367 00	12870 00	12870 00

10

JOURNAL

Date	Account Title and Explanation	Doc No.	Post. Ref.	General Debit	General Credit

Account Title: Supplies   **Account No.** 130

Date 20—	Explanation	Post. Ref.	Debit	Credit	Balance Debit	Balance Credit
July 1		✔			4319 00	

Account Title: Prepaid Insurance   **Account No.** 140

Date 20—	Explanation	Post. Ref.	Debit	Credit	Balance Debit	Balance Credit
July 1		✔			1600 00	

Account Title: Insurance Expense   **Account No.** 520

Date	Explanation	Post. Ref.	Debit	Credit	Balance Debit	Balance Credit

Account Title: Supplies Expense   **Account No.** 550

Date	Explanation	Post. Ref.	Debit	Credit	Balance Debit	Balance Credit

Review the material in this section in preparation for the Self Test. The Self Test will check your mastery of this particular section. The items missed on this Self Test will indicate specific areas where restudy is needed for mastery.

SELF TEST 1

Match the following accounting terms with their definitions (each answer, 2 points).

1.01 _____ occurs when total revenue is greater than total expenses

1.02 _____ informal papers in the form of memoranda, analysis papers, and informal reports

1.03 _____ the length of the accounting cycle for which a business summarizes and reports financial information

1.04 _____ a financial statement that reports the revenue and expenses for a fiscal period

1.05 _____ occurs when total expenses are greater than total revenue

1.06 _____ all revenue and expenses associated with a business activity are to be recorded in the same accounting period

1.07 _____ entries made in the journal to adjust the ledger accounts to contain the same balances as shown on the worksheet

1.08 _____ a financial statement that reports assets, liabilities and owner's equity on a specific date

1.09 _____ a columnar accounting form used to summarize the general ledger information needed to prepare financial statements

1.010 _____ an amount that is added to or subtracted from an account balance to bring the balance up to date

1.011 _____ delays the recognition of expenses or revenue until a later fiscal period

a. adjustment

b. balance sheet

c. matching expenses with revenue

d. fiscal period

e. income statement

f. net income

g. net loss

h. deferral adjustments

i. working papers

j. worksheet

k. adjusting entries

l. journalizing

1.012 **Journalize the worksheet adjustments** (34 points).

Use the information from the worksheet on the next page to journalize the worksheet adjustments for the **Floor-Shine Company**.

Floor-Shine Company
Worksheet
For the Month Ended November 30, 20—

ACCOUNT TITLE	TRIAL BALANCE DEBIT	TRIAL BALANCE CREDIT	ADJUSTMENTS DEBIT	ADJUSTMENTS CREDIT	INCOME STATEMENT DEBIT	INCOME STATEMENT CREDIT	BALANCE SHEET DEBIT	BALANCE SHEET CREDIT
Cash	5844 00						5844 00	
Petty Cash	300 00						300 00	
Supplies	1900 00			(a) 600 00			1300 00	
Prepaid Insurance	800 00			(b) 400 00			400 00	
Tyson Office Supply		166 00						166 00
Office Systems, Inc.		60 00						60 00
Mike Ford, Capital		8000 00						8000 00
Mike Ford, Drawing	560 00						560 00	
Sales		1628 00				1628 00		
Advertising Expense	75 00				75 00			
Insurance Expense			(b) 400 00		400 00			
Miscellaneous Expense	15 00				15 00			
Rent Expense	250 00				250 00			
Repair Expense	85 00				85 00			
Supplies Expense			(a) 600 00		600 00			
Utilities Expense	25 00				25 00			
Totals	9854 00	9854 00	1000 00	1000 00	1450 00	1628 00	8404 00	8226 00
Net Income					178 00			178 00
					1628 00	1628 00	8404 00	8404 00

	JOURNAL						Page 5	
Date	Account Title and Explanation	Doc No.	Post. Ref.	General Debit		General Credit		

1.013 **Post the adjusting entries for the Floor-Shine Company** (40 points).

Post the adjusting entries from the journal on the previous page. The ledger accounts are arranged in numerical order.

Account Title: *Supplies*   Account No. *130*

Date 20—		Explanation	Post. Ref.	Debit	Credit	Balance Debit	Balance Credit
Nov.	1		✔			1900 00	

Account Title: *Prepaid Insurance*   Account No. *140*

Date 20—		Explanation	Post. Ref.	Debit	Credit	Balance Debit	Balance Credit
Nov.	1		✔			800 00	

Account Title: *Insurance Expense*   Account No. *520*

Date		Explanation	Post. Ref.	Debit	Credit	Balance Debit	Balance Credit

Account Title: *Supplies Expense*   Account No. *560*

Date		Explanation	Post. Ref.	Debit	Credit	Balance Debit	Balance Credit

77 / 96

Score _____

Adult Check _____

Initial   Date

14

SECTION II. CLOSING ENTRIES

The Need for Closing Entries

After the financial statements are prepared for the fiscal period and adjusting entries have been recorded and posted, the books must be prepared for the next fiscal period. This preparation involves two types of accounts:

1. **Permanent Accounts** – accounts that accumulate financial information from one fiscal period to another,

2. **Temporary Accounts** – accounts that accumulate financial information until it is transferred to the owner's Capital account.

Permanent accounts (also called real accounts) are assets, liabilities, and the owner's Capital account for the business entity. These accounts normally will exist as long as the business entity exists. The ending balance of the permanent accounts of any fiscal period becomes the beginning balance of that account for the next fiscal period.

Temporary accounts (also known as nominal accounts) include revenue and expense accounts, the owner's Drawing account and the Income Summary account. The major function of the temporary accounts is to show changes in the owner's Capital account for a single accounting cycle. At the end of a fiscal period, the balances of the temporary accounts must be summarized and transferred to the owner's Capital account. All temporary accounts begin the new fiscal period with a zero balance.

A series of journal transactions is needed to transfer the balances of the temporary accounts to the owner's Capital account. These transactions are called **closing entries**. Closing entries are journal entries used to prepare temporary accounts for a new fiscal period. The temporary account balances must be transferred and their balances reduced to zero at the end of each fiscal period. This procedure prepares the temporary accounts for recording information for the next fiscal period. When a new fiscal period starts, revenue and expenses must be kept separate from any previous fiscal period. Otherwise, the amounts for the next fiscal period would be added to amounts for previous fiscal periods, making comparison impossible (Concept: Matching Expenses with Revenue). The net income from one fiscal period to the next would be difficult to calculate, thus producing inaccurate reports.

Closing entries also transfer the net income or net loss to the owner's Capital account. The net income or net loss is calculated on the worksheet. Then it is reported on the income statement. This net income or net loss is also reflected in the ending balance of Capital reported on the owner's equity statement. Then this ending Capital amount is transferred to the balance sheet and reported as the owner's equity for that date. However, none of the procedures involve recording of the amounts in the Capital account of the general ledger. The amounts represented by the owner's equity statement and the balance sheet do not agree with the general ledger. To have the amounts agree, closing entries must be recorded and posted.

There are four closing entries:

1. An entry to close all income statement accounts with credit balances (revenue).
2. An entry to close all income statement accounts with debit balances (expenses).
3. An entry to transfer the balance of Income Summary account (net income or net loss) to the owner's Capital account.
4. An entry to close the owner's Drawing account.

All information needed to record the four closing entries is found in the Income Statement and Balance Sheet columns of the worksheet.

The Income Summary Account

Prior to journalizing and posting closing entries, there is no single account in the general ledger that summarizes the revenue and expenses for the fiscal period. Information is recorded in several different accounts in the ledger and shown on the worksheet as individual items. The Income Summary account is the account that is used to summarize revenue and expenses for a fiscal period. Before closing, the Income Summary account should show the same net income or net loss as reported on the worksheet.

The Income Summary account serves several purposes:

1. It summarizes the revenue and expense information in the ledger, hence the name *Income Summary*.
2. It summarizes the total revenue and total expenses for each fiscal period.
3. It shows the net income/net loss for each fiscal period.
4. It allows one amount (either net income or net loss) to be entered in the owner's Capital account. This allows the Capital account to show only investments, withdrawals and net income or net loss for the fiscal period.

NOTE: Because of its effect on the Capital account, Income Summary falls under the same account number classification as the owner's Drawing account and thus is numbered in the 300 series. This temporary account does not become active until closing entries are made.

The Income Summary account is different from other ledger accounts because it does not have a consistent debit or credit balance. The balance is determined as the closing entries are posted to the account at the end of the accounting cycle. If the revenue for the period is larger than the expenses, resulting in a net income, the Income Summary account has a credit balance. If the expenses for the period are larger than the revenue, resulting in a net loss, the Income Summary account has a debit balance. In other words, business operations will determine whether the Income Summary account has a debit or a credit balance. Since Income Summary is also a temporary account, it must be closed at the end of the fiscal period.

Income Summary	
Left Side (Debit)	**Right Side (Credit)**
Expense Account Balances	Revenue Account Balances

Journalizing and Posting Closing Entries

Closing Entry for Revenue. The first closing entry is to transfer the balance of the revenue account to Income Summary. The purpose of this entry is to reduce the balance of the revenue account to zero. *Since revenue accounts have credit balances, the account(s) must be debited* in order to reduce the balance to zero. The information needed to record this transaction is found in the credit column of the income statement section of the worksheet for **The Craft Shop**, shown below.

The Craft Shop
Worksheet
For the Month Ended April 30, 20—

ACCOUNT TITLE	TRIAL BALANCE DEBIT	TRIAL BALANCE CREDIT	ADJUSTMENTS DEBIT	ADJUSTMENTS CREDIT	INCOME STATEMENT DEBIT	INCOME STATEMENT CREDIT	BALANCE SHEET DEBIT	BALANCE SHEET CREDIT
Cash	12454 00						12454 00	
Petty Cash	300 00						300 00	
Supplies	2950 00			(a)1849 00			1101 00	
Prepaid Insurance	3800 00			(b)1400 00			2400 00	
Jones Office Supply		1771 00						1771 00
Craft Supply, Inc.		1660 00						1660 00
J. Smith, Capital		13099 00						13099 00
J. Smith, Drawing	1560 00						1560 00	
Sales		8834 00				8834 00		
Advertising Expense	1775 00				1775 00			
Insurance Expense			(b)1400 00		1400 00			
Miscellaneous Expense	615 00				615 00			
Rent Expense	1000 00				1000 00			
Repair Expense	885 00				885 00			
Supplies Expense			(a)1849 00		1849 00			
Utilities Expense	25 00				25 00			
Totals	25364 00	25364 00	3249 00	3249 00	7549 00	8834 00	17815 00	16530 00
Net Income					1285 00			1285 00
					8834 00	8834 00	17815 00	17815 00

JOURNAL

Date 20—		Account Title and Explanation	Doc No.	Post. Ref.	General Debit		General Credit	
		Adjusting Entries						
Apr.	30	Supplies Expense			1849	00		
		Supplies					1849	00
	30	Insurance Expense			1400	00		
		Prepaid Insurance					1400	00
		1 *Closing Entries*						
2	30	Sales **3**			**4** 8834	00		
		5 Income Summary					**6** 8834	00

1. Enter the heading *Closing Entries* in the middle of the account title column of the journal. The heading should be entered on the line under the account title for the last adjustment. There is no need to skip a journal line. Using this heading eliminates the need for an explanation and a source document to verify the transaction.

2. Enter the date in the date column of the journal. This date represents the end of the fiscal period.

3. From the worksheet account title column (shown on the previous page), locate the revenue account for the first closing entry and write the account name, *Sales*, in the account title column of the journal.

4. Write the amount to be debited in the debit column of the journal. This amount is found in the income statement credit column. Sales has a credit balance. In order to reduce that balance to zero, Sales must be debited for $8,834.00.

5. Write the account title to be credited, *Income Summary*, on the next line.

6. Write the amount to be credited ($8,834.00) in the credit column of the journal.

Closing Entry for Expenses. The second closing entry is to transfer the balance of all the expense accounts to Income Summary. The purpose of this entry is to reduce the balance of all expense accounts to zero. *Since expense accounts have debit balances, the accounts must be credited* in order to reduce the balances to zero. The information needed to record these transactions is found in the debit column of the income statement section of the worksheet for **The Craft Shop**, shown below.

The Craft Shop
Worksheet
For the Month Ended April 30, 20—

ACCOUNT TITLE	TRIAL BALANCE		ADJUSTMENTS		INCOME STATEMENT		BALANCE SHEET	
	DEBIT	CREDIT	DEBIT	CREDIT	DEBIT	CREDIT	DEBIT	CREDIT
Cash	12454 00						12454 00	
Petty Cash	300 00						300 00	
Supplies	2950 00			(a)1849 00			1101 00	
Prepaid Insurance	3800 00			(b)1400 00			2400 00	
Jones Office Supply		1771 00						1771 00
Craft Supply, Inc.		1660 00						1660 00
J. Smith, Capital		13099 00						13099 00
J. Smith, Drawing	1560 00						1560 00	
Sales		8834 00				8834 00		
Advertising Expense	1775 00				1775 00			
Insurance Expense			(b)1400 00		1400 00			
Miscellaneous Expense	615 00				615 00			
Rent Expense	1000 00				1000 00			
Repair Expense	885 00				885 00			
Supplies Expense			(a)1849 00		1849 00			
Utilities Expense	25 00				25 00			
Totals	25364 00	25364 00	3249 00	3249 00	7549 00	8834 00	17815 00	16530 00
Net Income					1285 00			1285 00
					8834 00	8834 00	17815 00	17815 00

JOURNAL

Date 20—		Account Title and Explanation	Doc No.	Post. Ref.	General Debit		General Credit	
		Adjusting Entries						
Apr.	30	Supplies Expense		560	1849	00		
		Supplies		130			1849	00
	30	Insurance Expense		520	1400	00		
		Prepaid Insurance		140			1400	00
		Closing Entries						
	30	Sales		410	8834	00		
		Income Summary		330			8834	00
1	30	Income Summary 2			11 7549	00		
		3 Advertising Expense					4 1775	00
		5 Insurance Expense					1400	00
		6 Miscellaneous Expense					615	00
		7 Rent Expense					1000	00
		8 Repair Expense					885	00
		9 Supplies Expense					1849	00
		10 Utilities Expense					25	00

1. Enter the day (the last day of the fiscal period) in the date column of the journal.

2. Enter the account title, *Income Summary*, in the account title column of the journal. The debit amount for Income Summary will be determined later.

3. From the worksheet account title column, locate the expense accounts to be credited and enter the first expense account name, *Advertising Expense*, in the account title column of the journal. Be sure to indent this credit and all the remaining credits five spaces.

4. Enter the amount to be credited in the credit column of the journal. This amount is found in the income statement debit column. Since Advertising Expense has a *debit balance* of $1,775.00, reducing that balance to zero will require a *credit* of $1,775.00.

5. Enter the account name, *Insurance Expense*, in the account title column and credit the balance of that account in the same manner as Advertising Expense.

6. Enter the account name, *Miscellaneous Expense*, in the account title column and credit the balance of that account.

7. Enter the account name, *Rent Expense*, in the account title column of the journal and enter the balance of that account in the credit column of the journal.

8. Enter the account name, *Repair Expense*, in the account title column and credit the balance of that account.

9. Enter the account name, *Supplies Expense*, in the account title column and credit the balance of that account.

10. Enter the account name, *Utilities Expense*, in the account title column and credit the balance of that account.

11. To determine the amount to be debited to Income Summary, total the amount for all the expenses that were just credited. Income Summary should be debited for $1,775.00 + $1,400.00 + $615.00 + $1,000.00 + $885.00 + $1,849.00 + $25.00 = $7,549.00. This amount should agree with the subtotal of the debit column in the income statement section of the worksheet shown on page 19. Enter this amount as a debit to Income Summary.

Complete the following activity.

2.1 From the journal on the previous page, post the closing entries for **The Craft Shop** on the ledger accounts shown below. The closing entry for the Sales account has been done for you as an example. NOTE: The accounts are shown in the order in which they would appear in the ledger.

Account Title: *Income Summary*   **Account No.** 330

Date 20—	Explanation	Post. Ref.	Debit	Credit	Balance Debit	Balance Credit
Apr. 30		J2		8834 00		8834 00

Account Title: *Sales*   **Account No.** 410

Date 20—	Explanation	Post. Ref.	Debit	Credit	Balance Debit	Balance Credit
Apr. 15		J1		4450 00		4450 00
22		J1		4384 00		8834 00
30		J2	8834 00			——

Account Title: *Advertising Expense*   **Account No.** 510

Date 20—	Explanation	Post. Ref.	Debit	Credit	Balance Debit	Balance Credit
Apr. 3		J1	750 00		750 00	
16		J1	1025 00		1775 00	

Account Title: Insurance Expense   **Account No.** 520

Date 20—		Explanation	Post. Ref.	Debit		Credit		Balance			
								Debit		Credit	
Apr.	30		J2	1400	00			1400	00		

Account Title: Miscellaneous Expense   **Account No.** 530

Date 20—		Explanation	Post. Ref.	Debit		Credit		Balance			
								Debit		Credit	
Apr.	15		J1	615	00			615	00		

Account Title: Rent Expense   **Account No.** 540

Date 20—		Explanation	Post. Ref.	Debit		Credit		Balance			
								Debit		Credit	
Apr.	1		J1	1000	00			1000	00		

Account Title: Repair Expense   **Account No.** 550

Date 20—		Explanation	Post. Ref.	Debit		Credit		Balance			
								Debit		Credit	
Apr.	7		J1	800	00			800	00		
	24		J1	85	00			885	00		

Account Title: Supplies Expense   **Account No.** 560

Date 20—		Explanation	Post. Ref.	Debit		Credit		Balance			
								Debit		Credit	
Apr.	30		J2	1849	00			1849	00		

Account Title: *Utilities Expense*					Account No. *570*		
Date 20—	Explanation	Post. Ref.	Debit	Credit	Balance		
					Debit	Credit	
Apr. 12		J1	25 00		25 00		

Closing Entry for Income Summary. The third closing entry is to transfer the balance of the Income Summary account to the Capital account. The balance of the Income Summary account reflects the net income or net loss for the fiscal period. If the business incurred a net income during the fiscal period, the Income Summary account will have a credit balance. If there was a net loss, Income Summary will have a debit balance.

The partial journal pages below show the closing entry for the Income Summary account with a credit balance (net income) and with a debit balance (net loss).

Closing Entry for Income Summary with Net Income:

	30	Income Summary **2**			1285 00		
1		**3** Jane Smith, Capital				**4** 1285 00	

1. Enter the day (the last day of the fiscal period) in the date column of the journal.
2. Enter the account title, *Income Summary*, in the account title column of the journal. The Craft Shop had a net income of $1,285.00 for the fiscal period. This amount is the difference between the total expenses and the total revenue for the period and is shown as a *credit balance* in the Income Summary account. The balance of the Income Summary account is transferred to the owner's Capital account by *debiting* Income Summary for $1,285.00.
3. Write the account title to be credited, *Jane Smith, Capital*, on the next line.
4. Write the amount to be credited ($1,285.00) in the credit column of the journal.

Closing Entry for Income Summary with a Net Loss:

	30	Mike Fox, Capital **2**			1201 00		
1		**3** Income Summary				**4** 1201 00	

A business owned by Mike Fox had a net loss of $1,201.00 at the end of the fiscal period; therefore the Income Summary account will have a debit balance. Study the procedure on the following page to see how to close an Income Summary account with a net loss.

1. Enter the day (the last day of the fiscal period) in the date column of the journal.

2. Enter the account title, *Mike Fox, Capital*, in the account title column of the journal. The business had a net loss of $1,201.00 for the fiscal period. This amount is the difference between the total expenses and the total revenue for the period and is shown as a *debit balance* in the Income Summary account. The balance of the Income Summary account is transferred to the owner's Capital account by *crediting* Income Summary for $1,201.00.

3. Write the account title to be credited, *Income Summary*, on the next line.

4. Write the amount to be credited ($1,201.00) in the credit column of the journal.

Closing Entry for the Drawing Account. The owner's Drawing account is the last temporary account to be closed at the end of the fiscal period. The information for this closing entry comes from the debit column of the balance sheet section of the worksheet. Drawing, as you will recall, is withdrawals of cash from the business by the owner for personal use. Drawing decreases the owner's equity in the business. Decreases to the Capital account are shown as debits; therefore, the Drawing account has a debit balance.

Closing the Drawing account is the final step needed to bring the Capital account in the general ledger into agreement with two financial reports completed at the end of the fiscal period: the statement of owner's equity and the balance sheet.

The Craft Shop				
Statement of Owner's Equity				
For the Month Ended April 30, 20—				
Capital, April 1, 20—			13099	00
Add: Net Income			1285	00
Total			14384	00
Less: Withdrawals			1560	00
Jane Smith, Capital, April 30, 20—			12824	00

Notice that the statement of owner's equity shows the addition of net income to the balance of the Capital account. The closing entry for the Income Summary account reflected this addition in the general ledger. When you have journalized and posted the closing entry for the Drawing account, the Capital account in the ledger will accurately reflect Jane Smith's equity in her business at the end of the fiscal period.

The Craft Shop
Worksheet
For the Month Ended April 30, 20—

ACCOUNT TITLE	TRIAL BALANCE DEBIT	TRIAL BALANCE CREDIT	ADJUSTMENTS DEBIT	ADJUSTMENTS CREDIT	INCOME STATEMENT DEBIT	INCOME STATEMENT CREDIT	BALANCE SHEET DEBIT	BALANCE SHEET CREDIT
Cash	12454 00						12454 00	
Petty Cash	300 00						300 00	
Supplies	2950 00			(a)1849 00			1101 00	
Prepaid Insurance	3800 00			(b)1400 00			2400 00	
Jones Office Supply		1771 00						1771 00
Craft Supply, Inc.		1660 00						1660 00
J. Smith, Capital		13099 00						13099 00
J. Smith, Drawing	1560 00						1560 00	
Sales		8834 00				8834 00		
Advertising Expense	1775 00				1775 00			
Insurance Expense			(b)1400 00		1400 00			
Miscellaneous Expense	615 00				615 00			
Rent Expense	1000 00				1000 00			
Repair Expense	885 00				885 00			
Supplies Expense			(a)1849 00		1849 00			
Utilities Expense	25 00				25 00			
Totals	25364 00	25364 00	3249 00	3249 00	7549 00	8834 00	17815 00	16530 00
Net Income					1285 00			1285 00
					8834 00	8834 00	17815 00	17815 00

The partial journal page below shows the closing entry for the owner's Drawing account.

Closing Entry for Drawing Account:

1	30	Jane Smith, Capital	2			1560	00
		3 Jane Smith, Drawing				4 1560	00

1. Enter the day (the last day of the fiscal period) in the date column of the journal.
2. Enter the account title, *Jane Smith, Capital*, in the account title column of the journal. Decreases in capital are shown as a debit; therefore, the owner's Capital account will be debited for $1,560.00.
3. Write the account title to be credited, *Jane Smith, Drawing*, on the next line. This credit to Drawing will zero out the balance and close the account.
4. Write the amount to be credited ($1,560.00) in the credit column of the journal.

Journalize the adjusting and closing entries.

2.2 Mike Fox owns a business called **Fox Photography**. Use the worksheet shown below to journalize the adjusting and closing entries for the fiscal period ending March 31 of the current year.

Fox Photography
Worksheet
For the Month Ended March 31, 20—

ACCOUNT TITLE	TRIAL BALANCE DEBIT	TRIAL BALANCE CREDIT	ADJUSTMENTS DEBIT	ADJUSTMENTS CREDIT	INCOME STATEMENT DEBIT	INCOME STATEMENT CREDIT	BALANCE SHEET DEBIT	BALANCE SHEET CREDIT
Cash	10454 00						10454 00	
Petty Cash	300 00						300 00	
Supplies	4845 00			(a)2849 00			1996 00	
Prepaid Insurance	3800 00			(b)1400 00			2400 00	
Jones Office Supply		3666 00						3666 00
Maines Supplies, Inc.		1660 00						1660 00
Mike Fox, Capital		12585 00						12585 00
Mike Fox, Drawing	1560 00						1560 00	
Sales		8628 00				8628 00		
Advertising Expense	2775 00				2775 00			
Insurance Expense			(b)1400 00		1400 00			
Miscellaneous Expense	615 00				615 00			
Rent Expense	1280 00				1280 00			
Repair Expense	885 00				885 00			
Supplies Expense			(a)2849 00		2849 00			
Utilities Expense	25 00				25 00			
Totals	26539 00	26539 00	4249 00	4249 00	9829 00	8628 00	16710 00	17911 00
Net Loss						1201 00	1201 00	
					9829 00	9829 00	17911 00	17911 00

Date		Account Title and Explanation	Doc No.	Post. Ref.	General Debit		General Credit	

Review

- **To close any revenue account**, credit Income Summary for the total amount of revenue reported on the worksheet. Debit the revenue account for the amount of its balance.

- **To close the expense accounts**, debit Income Summary for the total amount of all expenses. Credit each individual expense for the amount of its balance.

- **To close the Income Summary account if there is a net income**, debit Income Summary for the amount of the Net Income. Credit the owner's Capital account for the value of the net income.

- **To close the Income Summary account if there is a net loss**, credit Income Summary for the amount of the net loss. Debit the owner's Capital account for the value of the net loss.

- **To close the Drawing account**, credit the Drawing account for the amount equal to its balance. Debit Capital for the balance of the Drawing account.

- **Closing entries are made for the temporary capital accounts only**. These accounts are revenue, expenses, income summary, and the owner's Drawing account.

- **Permanent accounts are never closed**. Their balances are carried over to the next fiscal period. These accounts are assets, liabilities and owner's equity (Capital).

Review the material in this section in preparation for the Self Test. This Self Test will check your mastery of this particular section as well as your knowledge of the previous section.

SELF TEST 2

Complete these activities (each answer, 2 points).

2.01   Why are closing entries needed?

_____

_____

_____

2.02   What are the four types of temporary accounts?

a. _____   b. _____

c. _____   d. _____

2.03   Describe the four closing entries.

a. _____

b. _____

c. _____

d. _____

2.04   To close the revenue account, Sales, which account must be debited and which account must be credited?

Debit: _____

Credit: _____

2.05   To close the expense account, Advertising Expense, which account must be debited and which account must be credited?

Debit: _____

Credit: _____

2.06   To close the Income Summary Account showing a *net income*, which account must be debited and which account must be credited?

Debit: _____

Credit: _____

2.07   To close the Income Summary Account showing a *net loss*, which account must be debited and which account must be credited?

Debit: _____

Credit: _____

2.08   To close the Owner's Drawing Account, which account must be debited and which account must be credited?

Debit: _____

Credit: _____

2.09   What are real or permanent accounts?

_____

_____

Journalize the adjusting and closing entries (45 points).

2.010 Durwood Lawson owns a business called **Lawson's Lawn Service**. Shown below is his worksheet for the fiscal period ending July 31 of the current year. Use the journal form on the following page to journalize the adjusting and closing entries. Begin your entries on page 1 of the journal.

Lawson's Lawn Service
Worksheet
For the Month Ended July 31, 20—

ACCOUNT TITLE	TRIAL BALANCE DEBIT	TRIAL BALANCE CREDIT	ADJUSTMENTS DEBIT	ADJUSTMENTS CREDIT	INCOME STATEMENT DEBIT	INCOME STATEMENT CREDIT	BALANCE SHEET DEBIT	BALANCE SHEET CREDIT
Cash	7822 00						7822 00	
Petty Cash	300 00						300 00	
Supplies	4319 00			(a) 1008 00			3311 00	
Prepaid Insurance	1600 00			(b) 150 00			1450 00	
John's Garage		1630 00						1630 00
Wick Supplies		300 00						300 00
D. Lawson, Capital		9000 00						9000 00
D. Lawson, Drawing	500 00						500 00	
Sales		4367 00				4367 00		
Advertising Expense	86 00				86 00			
Insurance Expense			(b) 150 00		150 00			
Miscellaneous Expense	95 00				95 00			
Rent Expense	450 00				450 00			
Supplies Expense			(a) 1008 00		1008 00			
Utilities Expense	125 00				125 00			
Totals	15297 00	15297 00	1158 00	1158 00	1914 00	4367 00	13383 00	10930 00
Net Income					2453 00			2453 00
					4367 00	4367 00	13383 00	13383 00

30

JOURNAL

Page

Date	Account Title and Explanation	Doc No.	Post. Ref.	General Debit		General Credit	

68 / 85

Score _____

Adult Check _____

Initial   Date

SECTION III. POST-CLOSING TRIAL BALANCE

The Purpose of the Post-Closing Trial Balance

The post-closing trial balance does the following:

1. It lists only open permanent accounts. The permanent accounts that remain open from fiscal period to fiscal period are assets, liabilities and the owner's equity capital account.

2. It contains no temporary accounts. In the previous section you learned how to close the temporary accounts (expenses, revenue and drawing) and how to transfer those account balances to Income Summary and, ultimately, to the owner's Capital account. This was done in order to keep revenue and expenses within the same fiscal period (matching expenses with revenue).

3. It contains the accounts and their balances that agree completely with the items on the balance sheet.

4. It verifies that the ledger is now ready to receive the entries for the new accounting period. It proves the equality of the debits and credits in the general ledger after closing entries have been made.

Preparing a Post-Closing Trial Balance

The only difference between a post-closing trial balance and a formal trial balance is the absence of the temporary accounts. Only the accounts that have balances (the permanent accounts) are listed on the post-closing trial balance. These accounts and their balances should be the same as shown on the balance sheet prepared at the end of the fiscal period.

The Craft Shop
Post-Closing Trial Balance
April 30, 20—

ACCOUNT TITLE	ACCT. NO.	DEBIT		CREDIT	
Cash	110	12454	00		
Petty Cash	120	300	00		
Supplies	130	1101	00		
Prepaid Insurance	140	2400	00		
Jones Office Supply	210			1771	00
Craft Supply, Inc.	220			1660	00
Jane Smith, Capital	310			12824	00
Totals		16255	00	16255	00

1. The heading section must provide the name of the business entity, the name of the financial statement and the fiscal period represented (the three W's: *Who*, *What* and *When*). Notice the specific date—the last day of the fiscal period.

2. In the account title column, write the account titles, account numbers and the debit or credit balance of all general ledger accounts that are still open after the closing entries have been made.

3. Rule a single line across both columns below the last entry and total the columns. They must be equal.

4. Write the word *Totals* on the line below the last account title.

5. Rule double lines across both amount columns to indicate that the totals are correct and balanced.

Complete the following activity.

3.1 Joanne Clever owns a business called **Clever Closet Company**. Shown below are her general ledger accounts after adjusting and closing entries have been posted. Prepare a post-closing trial balance for Clever Closet Company for May 31 of the current year.

Account Title: *Cash*   **Account No.** *110*

Date 20—		Explanation	Post. Ref.	Debit		Credit		Balance Debit		Balance Credit	
May	1		✔					11925	00		
	12		J1	939	00			12864	00		
	21		J1			55	00	12809	00		
	26		J1	942	00			13751	00		
	30		J1			430	00	13321	00		

Account Title: *Petty Cash*   **Account No.** *120*

Date 20—		Explanation	Post. Ref.	Debit		Credit		Balance Debit		Balance Credit	
May	1		✔					300	00		

Account Title: *Supplies*   **Account No.** *130*

Date 20—		Explanation	Post. Ref.	Debit		Credit		Balance Debit		Balance Credit	
May	1		✔					1280	00		
	10		J1	1422	00			2702	00		
	14		J1	1198	00			3900	00		
	31		J2			1700	00	2200	00		

Account Title: *Prepaid Insurance*   **Account No.** *140*

Date 20—		Explanation	Post. Ref.	Debit		Credit		Balance Debit		Balance Credit	
May	1		✔					1200	00		
	31		J2			300	00	900	00		

ACCOUNTING

seven

LIFEPAC TEST

104 / 130

Name _____

Date _____

Score _____

LIFEPAC TEST ACCOUNTING 7

PART I

On the blank, print a *T* if the statement is true or an *F* if the statement is false (each answer, 1 point).

1. _____ Adjusting entries are used to correct errors made in journalizing and posting transactions during a fiscal period.

2. _____ Balances of the temporary accounts should be carried forward to the next fiscal period.

3. _____ After the closing entries are recorded and posted, a post-closing trial balance is prepared.

4. _____ The balances of the permanent accounts are always carried forward to the next fiscal period.

5. _____ Adjusting entries are made to bring accounts up to date.

6. _____ Assets/expense adjustments are adjustments done on the worksheet to transfer the expended portion of an asset account to an expense account.

7. _____ The income summary account is always closed by debiting the account.

8. _____ The balance sheet is completed before the statement of owner's equity.

9. _____ The worksheet is always prepared in ink because it is part of the official financial records of a business.

10. _____ The date of all financial statements is preceded by the phrase, "For the Month Ended."

For each statement below, circle the letter of the choice that best completes the sentence (each answer, 1 point).

11. The second line on the heading of a worksheet is:
    a. the name of the report
    b. the name of the business
    c. the current fiscal period
    d. the current date

12. Income Summary account is classified as:
    a. a liability account   b. an asset account
    c. a temporary capital account   d. a revenue account

13. The purpose of the post-closing trial balance is:
    a. to prove accuracy of the general ledger account balances after the closing entries are posted
    b. to prove the accuracy of the general ledger accounts after journalizing and posting all transactions
    c. to bring certain general ledger accounts up to date
    d. to analyze the debit and credit of each adjusting entry

1

14. The amount of supplies used during a fiscal period is transferred to:
    a. an asset account
    b. a liability account
    c. an expense account
    d. a revenue account

15. During the closing process, a net income is transferred to:
    a. the balance sheet
    b. the debit side of Income Summary
    c. the owner's Drawing account
    d. the owner's Capital account

16. The source of information to record the adjusting entries is found in the:
    a. worksheet's adjustment column
    b. worksheet's trial balance columns
    c. general ledger
    d. worksheet's income statement columns

17. During the closing process, a net loss is first shown:
    a. on the balance sheet
    b. as a debit balance in Income Summary
    c. in the owner's Capital account
    d. in the owner's Drawing account

18. The source of information to record the closing entries is found in the:
    a. worksheet's adjustment columns
    b. worksheet's trial balance columns
    c. worksheet's adjusted trial balance columns
    d. worksheet's income statement columns

19. The account debited to close any revenue account is:
    a. the owner's Capital account
    b. the Income Summary account
    c. the owner's Drawing account
    d. the revenue account

20. The account credited to adjust the Prepaid Insurance account is:
    a. Prepaid Insurance
    b. Insurance Expense
    c. Income Summary
    d. the owner's Drawing account

21. The third required closing entry is:
    a. close revenue to Income Summary
    b. close Income Summary to Capital
    c. close expenses to Income Summary
    d. close Drawing to Capital

22. The owner's Capital account listed on the post-closing trial balance should have the same balance as shown on the:
    a. worksheet's trial balance columns
    b. worksheet's balance sheet columns
    c. the balance sheet
    d. worksheet's adjustment columns

23. The account debited to adjust the Prepaid Insurance account is:
    a. Prepaid Insurance
    b. Insurance Expense
    c. Income Summary
    d. the owner's Drawing account

24. The first required closing entry is:
    a. close revenue to Income Summary
    b. close Income Summary to Capital
    c. close expenses to Income Summary
    d. close Drawing to Capital

25. The fourth required closing entry is:
    a. close revenue to Income Summary
    b. close Income Summary to Capital
    c. close expenses to Income Summary
    d. close Drawing to Capital

26. The balance of the Supplies account (after the closing entries are posted) represents:
   a. the supplies used
   b. the supplies on hand
   c. supplies purchased on account
   d. all supplies purchased

27. The second required closing entry is:
   a. close revenue to Income Summary
   b. close Income Summary to Capital
   c. close expenses to Income Summary
   d. close Drawing to Capital

Match the following accounting terms with their definitions (each answer, 1 point).

28. _____ a financial statement that reports the revenue and expenses for a fiscal period

29. _____ occurs when total expenses are greater than total revenue

30. _____ a form completed after closing that checks the equality of debits and credits in the general ledger

31. _____ entries prepared at the end of a fiscal period to transfer the balances of temporary accounts to the owner's Capital account

32. _____ occurs when total revenue is greater than total expenses

33. _____ entries made in the journal to adjust the ledger accounts to contain the same balances as shown on the worksheet

34. _____ "nominal" accounts

35. _____ all revenue and expenses for a business activity are recorded in the same accounting period

36. _____ the length of the accounting cycle for which a business summarizes and reports financial information

37. _____ an amount that is added to or subtracted from an account balance to bring the balance up to date

38. _____ delays the recognition of expenses or revenue until a later fiscal period

39. _____ the same accounting concepts are applied the same way for each fiscal period

40. _____ "real" accounts

a. net loss

b. adjustment

c. temporary accounts

d. permanent accounts

e. matching expenses with revenue

f. consistent reporting

g. worksheet

h. working papers

i. closing entries

j. fiscal period

k. net income

l. deferral adjustments

m. post-closing trial balance

n. adjusting entries

o. income statement

Complete this activity (each answer, 1 point).

41. For each account title listed, place an X in the proper columns to show if the account is affected by adjusting or closing entries and whether or not it appears on the post-closing trial balance.

Account Title	Account adjusted from adjusting entries?		Account closed during closing procedure?		Account appears on the post-closing trial balance?	
	YES	NO	YES	NO	YES	NO
Cash						
Office Max						
Owner's Capital						
Owner's Drawing						
Sales						
Advertising Expense						
Insurance Expense						
Prepaid Insurance						
Rent Expense						
Supplies						
Supplies Expense						
Utilities Expense						
Commissions						
Petty Cash						
Mortgage Payable						

PART II

42. From the worksheet below, record the adjusting and closing entries on page 2 of the general journal form provided.

Davis Enterprises
Worksheet
For the Month Ended September 30, 20—

ACCOUNT TITLE	TRIAL BALANCE DEBIT	TRIAL BALANCE CREDIT	ADJUSTMENTS DEBIT	ADJUSTMENTS CREDIT	INCOME STATEMENT DEBIT	INCOME STATEMENT CREDIT	BALANCE SHEET DEBIT	BALANCE SHEET CREDIT
Cash	7782 00						7782 00	
Petty Cash	300 00						300 00	
Supplies	4319 00			(a) 1341 00			2978 00	
Prepaid Insurance	1600 00			(b) 330 00			1270 00	
Office Max		1630 00						1630 00
Wick Supplies		300 00						300 00
Jan Davis, Capital		9000 00						9000 00
Jan Davis, Drawing	500 00						500 00	
Sales		4327 00				4327 00		
Advertising Expense	86 00				86 00			
Insurance Expense			(b) 330 00		330 00			
Miscellaneous Expense	95 00				95 00			
Rent Expense	450 00				450 00			
Supplies Expense			(a) 1341 00		1341 00			
Utilities Expense	125 00				125 00			
Totals	15257 00	15257 00	1671 00	1671 00	2427 00	4327 00	12830 00	10930 00
Net Income					1900 00			1900 00
					4327 00	4327 00	12830 00	12830 00

5

Date	Account Title and Explanation	Doc No.	Post. Ref.	General Debit		General Credit	

JOURNAL

Page

NOTES

Account Title: Tyson Office Supply   **Account No.** 210

Date 20—		Explanation	Post. Ref.	Debit		Credit		Balance Debit		Balance Credit	
May	1		✔							1466	00
	13		J1	300	00					1166	00

Account Title: Office Systems, Inc.   **Account No.** 220

Date 20—		Explanation	Post. Ref.	20—Debit		Credit		Balance Debit		Balance Credit	
May	1		✔							1060	00
	14		J1	100	00					960	00

Account Title: Joanne Clever, Capital   **Account No.** 310

Date 20—		Explanation	Post. Ref.	Debit		Credit		Balance Debit		Balance Credit	
May	1		✔							15000	00
	31		J2			455	00			15455	00
	31		J2	860	00					14595	00

Account Title: Joanne Clever, Drawing   **Account No.** 320

Date 20—		Explanation	Post. Ref.	Debit		Credit		Balance Debit		Balance Credit	
May	15		J1	430	00			430	00		
	30		J1	430	00			860	00		
	31		J2			860	00	———			

Account Title: Income Summary   **Account No.** 330

Date 20—		Explanation	Post. Ref.	Debit		Credit		Balance Debit		Balance Credit	
May	31		J2			3675	00			3675	00
	31		J2	3220	00					455	00
	31		J2	455	00					———	

Account Title: Sales   **Account No.** 410

Date 20—		Explanation	Post. Ref.	Debit		Credit		Balance Debit		Balance Credit	
May	7		J1			919	00			919	00
	14		J1			875	00			1794	00
	21		J1			939	00			2733	00
	26		J1			942	00			3675	00
	31		J2	3675	00					——	

Account Title: Advertising Expense   **Account No.** 510

Date 20—		Explanation	Post. Ref.	Debit		Credit		Balance Debit		Balance Credit	
May	1		J1	75	00			75	00		
	9		J1	100	00			175	00		
	31		J2			175	00	——			

Account Title: Insurance Expense   **Account No.** 520

Date 20—		Explanation	Post. Ref.	Debit		Credit		Balance Debit		Balance Credit	
May	31		J2	300	00			300	00		
	31		J2			300	00	——			

Account Title: Miscellaneous Expense   **Account No.** 530

Date 20—		Explanation	Post. Ref.	Debit		Credit		Balance Debit		Balance Credit	
May	6		J1	40	00			40	00		
	14		J1	45	00			85	00		
	31		J2			85	00	——			

Account Title: Rent Expense   **Account No.** 540

Date 20—		Explanation	Post. Ref.	Debit		Credit		Balance Debit		Balance Credit	
May	1		J1	550	00			550	00		
	31		J2			550	00	——			

Account Title: Repair Expense — Account No. 550

Date 20—		Explanation	Post. Ref.	Debit		Credit		Balance Debit		Balance Credit	
May	16		J1	285	00			285	00		
	31		J2			285	00	—	—		

Account Title: Supplies Expense — Account No. 560

Date 20—		Explanation	Post. Ref.	Debit		Credit		Balance Debit		Balance Credit	
May	31		J2	1700	00			1700	00		
	31		J2			1700	00	—	—		

Account Title: Utilities Expense — Account No. 570

Date 20—		Explanation	Post. Ref.	Debit		Credit		Balance Debit		Balance Credit	
May	10		J1	70	00			70	00		
	21		J1	55	00			125	00		
	31		J2			125	00	—	—		

ACCOUNT TITLE	ACCT. NO.	DEBIT	CREDIT

Review the material in this section in preparation for the Self Test. This Self Test will check your mastery of this particular section as well as your knowledge of the previous sections.

SELF TEST 3

Match the following accounting terms with their definitions (each answer, 2 points).

3.01 _____ a financial statement that reports the revenue and expenses for a fiscal period

3.02 _____ occurs when total expenses are greater than total revenue

3.03 _____ a form completed after closing that checks the equality of debits and credits in the general ledger

3.04 _____ entries prepared at the end of a fiscal period to transfer the balances of temporary accounts to the owner's Capital account

3.05 _____ occurs when total revenue is greater than total expenses

3.06 _____ entries made in the journal to adjust the ledger accounts to contain the same balances as shown on the worksheet

3.07 _____ "nominal" accounts

3.08 _____ all revenue and expenses for a business activity are recorded in the same accounting period

3.09 _____ the length of the accounting cycle for which a business summarizes and reports financial information

3.010 _____ an amount that is added to or subtracted from an account balance to bring the balance up to date

3.011 _____ delays the recognition of expenses or revenue until a later fiscal period

3.012 _____ the same accounting concepts are applied the same way for each fiscal period

3.013 _____ "real" accounts

a. adjustment

b. temporary accounts

c. matching expenses with revenue

d. closing entries

e. fiscal period

f. income statement

g. net income

h. net loss

i. deferral adjustments

j. permanent accounts

k. post-closing trial balance

l. worksheet

m. adjusting entries

n. consistent reporting

o. working papers

Complete this activity (each answer, 3 points).

3.014 Number the following *adjusting* and *closing* journal entries in their correct order.

_____ Transfer the balance of the Income Summary account to the owner's Capital account.

_____ Transfer the expense account balances to the Income Summary account.

_____ Transfer the balance of the owner's Drawing account to the Capital account.

_____ Update the balances of the Supplies and Prepaid Insurance accounts.

_____ Transfer the revenue account balances to the Income Summary account.

Complete this activity (each answer, 1 point).

3.015 For each account title listed, place an X in the proper columns to show if the account is affected by adjusting or closing entries and whether or not it appears on the post-closing trial balance.

Account Title	Account adjusted from adjusting entries?		Account closed during closing procedure?		Account appears on the Post-Closing Trial Balance?	
	YES	NO	YES	NO	YES	NO
Cash						
Utilities Expense						
Office Max (Liability)						
Advertising Expense						
Petty Cash						
Commission Income						
John Jones, Capital						
Insurance Expense						
Supplies						
Supplies Expense						
Prepaid Insurance						
John Jones, Drawing						
Rent Expense						
NBT Bank (Liability)						
Income Summary						
Sales Revenue						
Misc. Expense						
Equipment						
Law Library						

SECTION IV. REVIEW & APPLICATION PROBLEMS

Summary

1. The major function of the worksheet as an accounting tool is to show the effects of the adjustments on general ledger accounts. It is also used to organize the data for use in preparing financial statements and recording the adjusting and closing entries.

2. It is a common practice for many businesses to pay cash for expenses in one fiscal period, but the expense is not used until a later fiscal period (deferral adjustments). Therefore an adjustment is needed to bring the accounts up to date at the end of a fiscal period.

3. The Adjustment section of the worksheet is the source of information for recording adjusting entries.

4. After the adjusting entries are journalized, they are posted to the general ledger.

5. There are two types of general ledger accounts: (1) Permanent Accounts—assets, liabilities, and the owner's Capital account—that accumulate financial information from one fiscal period to another, and (2) Temporary Accounts—revenue, expenses, income summary, and the owner's Drawing account—that accumulate financial information until it is transferred to the owner's Capital account.

6. The closing entries transfer the balances of the temporary capital accounts to the owner's Capital account. The Income Statement section of the worksheet is the source for the balances of the temporary accounts.

7. Only temporary accounts (revenue and expense accounts, the Income Summary account and the owner's Drawing account) are closed.

8. The four closing entries are: (1) an entry to close all income statement accounts with credit balances (revenue accounts), (2) an entry to close all income statement accounts with debit balances (expense accounts), (3) an entry to transfer the balance of Income Summary account (net income or net loss) to the owner's Capital account, and (4) an entry to close the owner's Drawing account.

9. After closing entries are recorded, they are posted to the general ledger accounts. The general ledger is then ready for use in the next fiscal period.

10. A post-closing trial balance is prepared after the closing entries are posted.

11. The basic steps in the accounting cycle are: (1) analyze each business transaction to see which accounts are affected, (2) journalize the transactions, (3) post the journal entries to the general ledger accounts and prepare a trial balance, (5) complete the worksheet and prepare financial statements, (6) record and post the adjusting entries, (7) record and post the closing entries, and (8) prepare a post-closing trial balance.

Complete the following activities.

4.1 Use the partial worksheet below to record the adjusting entries on page 3 of the general journal. (NOTE: only the accounts needed for this exercise are shown.) The entries are to be recorded as of July 31 of the current year.

ACCOUNT NAME	ADJUSTMENTS	
	DEBIT	CREDIT
Supplies – Office		(a) 600 00
Supplies – Store		(b) 850 00
Prepaid Insurance		(c) 900 00
Insurance Expense	(c) 900 00	
Supplies Expense – Office	(a) 600 00	
Supplies Expense – Store	(b) 850 00	

JOURNAL   Page

Date	Account Title and Explanation	Doc No.	Post. Ref.	General Debit	General Credit

4.2 Post the adjusting entries for exercise 4.1 to the general ledger. (NOTE: only the accounts needed for this exercise are shown.)

Account Title: Supplies – Office   **Account No.** 130

Date 20—	Explanation	Post. Ref.	Debit	Credit	Balance Debit	Balance Credit
July 1		✔			800 00	
10		J1	400 00		1200 00	
21		J2	450 00		1650 00	

41

Account Title: Supplies – Store   **Account No.** 140

Date 20—		Explanation	Post. Ref.	Debit		Credit		Balance Debit		Balance Credit	
July	1		✔					1850	00		
	15		J1	250	00			2100	00		
	25		J2	680	00			2780	00		

Account Title: Prepaid Insurance   **Account No.** 150

Date 20—		Explanation	Post. Ref.	Debit		Credit		Balance Debit		Balance Credit	
July	1		✔					800	00		
	15		J1	1200	00			2000	00		

Account Title: Insurance Expense   **Account No.** 520

Date		Explanation	Post. Ref.	Debit		Credit		Balance Debit		Balance Credit	

Account Title: Supplies Expense – Office   **Account No.** 530

Date		Explanation	Post. Ref.	Debit		Credit		Balance Debit		Balance Credit	

Account Title: Supplies Expense – Store   **Account No.** 540

Date		Explanation	Post. Ref.	Debit		Credit		Balance Debit		Balance Credit	

Complete the following activities.

4.3   From the partial worksheet, record the closing entries in the general journal below. Adjusting entries have already been recorded and posted. Date the closing entries July 31.

ACCOUNT NAME	INCOME STATEMENT		BALANCE SHEET	
	DEBIT	CREDIT	DEBIT	CREDIT
John Harrison, Capital				10960 00
John Harrison, Drawing			1200 00	
Sales		11160 00		
Advertising Expense	3450 00			
Credit Card Fee Expense	260 00			
Insurance Expense	220 00			
Miscellaneous Expense	380 00			
Rent Expense	1200 00			
Salary Expense	1900 00			
Supplies Expense – Office	480 00			
Supplies Expense – Store	380 00			
Totals	8270 00	11160 00	22050 00	19160 00
Net Income	2890 00			2890 00
	11160 00	11160 00	22050 00	22050 00

JOURNAL
Page 3

Date 20—		Account Title and Explanation	Doc No.	Post. Ref.	General Debit		General Credit	

4.4   Use the following ledger accounts to post the closing entries from exercise 4.3.

Account Title: John Harrison, Capital   **Account No.** 310

Date 20—		Explanation	Post. Ref.	Debit		Credit		Balance			
								Debit		Credit	
July	1		✔							10960	00

Account Title: John Harrison, Drawing   **Account No.** 320

Date 20—		Explanation	Post. Ref.	Debit		Credit		Balance			
								Debit		Credit	
July	15		J1	600	00			600	00		
	30		J1	600	00			1200	00		

Account Title: Income Summary   **Account No.** 330

Date		Explanation	Post. Ref.	Debit		Credit		Balance			
								Debit		Credit	

Account Title: Sales   **Account No.** 410

Date 20—		Explanation	Post. Ref.	Debit		Credit		Balance			
								Debit		Credit	
July	7		J1			2790	00			2790	00
	14		J1			2000	00			4790	00
	21		J2			2370	00			7160	00
	30		J2			4000	00			11160	00

Account Title: Advertising Expense   **Account No.** 510

Date 20—		Explanation	Post. Ref.	Debit		Credit		Balance Debit		Credit	
July	5		J1	1450	00			1450	00		
	15		J1	1200	00			2650	00		
	20		J2	800	00			3450	00		

Account Title: Credit Card Fee Expense   **Account No.** 520

Date 20—		Explanation	Post. Ref.	Debit		Credit		Balance Debit		Credit	
July	25		J2	260	00			260	00		

Account Title: Insurance Expense   **Account No.** 530

Date 20—		Explanation	Post. Ref.	Debit		Credit		Balance Debit		Credit	
July	31		J2	220	00			220	00		

Account Title: Miscellaneous Expense   **Account No.** 540

Date 20—		Explanation	Post. Ref.	Debit		Credit		Balance Debit		Credit	
July	6		J1	180	00			180	00		
	10		J1	200	00			380	00		

Account Title: Rent Expense   **Account No.** 550

Date 20—		Explanation	Post. Ref.	Debit		Credit		Balance Debit		Credit	
July	1		J1	1200	00			1200	00		

Account Title: Salary Expense   Account No. 560

Date 20—		Explanation	Post. Ref.	Debit		Credit		Balance Debit		Credit	
July	14		J1	950	00			950	00		
	28		J2	950	00			1900	00		

Account Title: Supplies Expense – Office   Account No. 570

Date 20—		Explanation	Post. Ref.	Debit		Credit		Balance Debit		Credit	
July	31		J3	480	00			480	00		

Account Title: Supplies Expense – Store   Account No. 580

Date 20—		Explanation	Post. Ref.	Debit		Credit		Balance Debit		Credit	
July	31		J3	380	00			380	00		

Complete the following activity.

4.5　From the partial worksheet below, record the closing entries on page 2 of the general journal. The entries should be dated September 30 of the current year.

ACCOUNT NAME	INCOME STATEMENT		BALANCE SHEET	
	DEBIT	CREDIT	DEBIT	CREDIT
Rufus Hartman, Capital				12795 00
Rufus Hartman, Drawing			950 00	
Commissions		5200 00		
Advertising Expense	290 00			
Insurance Expense	500 00			
Miscellaneous Expense	480 00			
Rent Expense	1800 00			
Supplies Expense – Office	560 00			
Supplies Expense – Store	440 00			
Utilities Expense	340 00			
Totals	4410 00	5200 00	12950 00	12160 00
Net Income	790 00			790 00
	5200 00	5200 00	12950 00	12950 00

JOURNAL　　　　Page

Date	Account Title and Explanation	Doc No.	Post. Ref.	General Debit	General Credit

Complete the following activities.

Donna Howard owns a business called **Howard's Florist**. The general ledger for Howard's Florist is shown on the following pages. (NOTE: Only the balances are shown to simulate the end of the monthly fiscal period, ended on November 30 of the current year.)

4.6 **Prepare a trial balance on the worksheet provided and complete the worksheet.** Use the following information to make the adjustments to update these accounts:

Inventory for Office Supplies on Nov. 30 – $450.00

Inventory for Store Supplies on Nov. 30 – $250.00

Value of Prepaid Insurance on Nov. 30 – $340.00

4.7 **Record and post the adjusting entries** on page 4 of a general journal.

4.8 **Record and post the closing entries** on page 4 of a general journal.

4.9 **Prepare a post-closing trial balance**.

Account Title: *Cash*					Account No. *110*	
Date 20—	Explanation	Post. Ref.	Debit	Credit	Balance Debit	Balance Credit
Nov. 30		✔			3600 00	

Account Title: *Petty Cash*					Account No. *120*	
Date 20—	Explanation	Post. Ref.	Debit	Credit	Balance Debit	Balance Credit
Nov. 30		✔			300 00	

Account Title: Office Supplies — Account No. 130

Date 20—		Explanation	Post. Ref.	Debit		Credit		Balance Debit		Balance Credit	
Nov.	30		✔					950	00		

Account Title: Store Supplies — Account No. 140

Date 20—		Explanation	Post. Ref.	Debit		Credit		Balance Debit		Balance Credit	
Nov.	30		✔					850	00		

Account Title: Prepaid Insurance — Account No. 150

Date 20—		Explanation	Post. Ref.	Debit		Credit		Balance Debit		Balance Credit	
Nov.	30		✔					540	00		

Account Title: Equipment — Account No. 160

Date 20—		Explanation	Post. Ref.	Debit		Credit		Balance Debit		Balance Credit	
Nov.	30		✔					7595	00		

Account Title: Bern Company — Account No. 210

Date 20—		Explanation	Post. Ref.	Debit		Credit		Balance Debit		Balance Credit	
Nov.	30		✔							500	00

Account Title: Kelly Company **Account No.** 220

Date 20—		Explanation	Post. Ref.	Debit		Credit		Balance			
								Debit		**Credit**	
Nov.	30		✔							120	00

Account Title: Donna Howard, Capital **Account No.** 310

Date 20—		Explanation	Post. Ref.	Debit		Credit		Balance			
								Debit		**Credit**	
Nov.	30		✔							12765	00

Account Title: Donna Howard, Drawing **Account No.** 320

Date 20—		Explanation	Post. Ref.	Debit		Credit		Balance			
								Debit		**Credit**	
Nov.	30		✔	550	00			550	00		

Account Title: Income Summary **Account No.** 330

Date 20—		Explanation	Post. Ref.	Debit		Credit		Balance			
								Debit		**Credit**	

Account Title: Sales **Account No.** 410

Date 20—		Explanation	Post. Ref.	Debit		Credit		Balance			
								Debit		**Credit**	
Nov.	30		✔							2300	00

Account Title: *Advertising Expense*   **Account No.** *510*

Date 20—		Explanation	Post. Ref.	Debit	Credit	Balance Debit	Balance Credit
Nov.	30		✔			600 00	

Account Title: *Insurance Expense*   **Account No.** *520*

Date 20—		Explanation	Post. Ref.	Debit	Credit	Balance Debit	Balance Credit

Account Title: *Miscellaneous Expense*   **Account No.** *530*

Date 20—		Explanation	Post. Ref.	Debit	Credit	Balance Debit	Balance Credit
Nov.	30		✔			185 00	

Account Title: *Rent Expense*   **Account No.** *540*

Date 20—		Explanation	Post. Ref.	Debit	Credit	Balance Debit	Balance Credit
Nov.	30		✔			425 00	

Account Title: *Repair Expense*   **Account No.** *550*

Date 20—		Explanation	Post. Ref.	Debit	Credit	Balance Debit	Balance Credit
Nov.	30		✔			90 00	

Account Title: *Supplies Expense – Office*					Account No. *560*	
Date 20—	Explanation	Post. Ref.	Debit	Credit	Balance	
					Debit	Credit

Account Title: *Supplies Expense – Store*					Account No. *570*	
Date 20—	Explanation	Post. Ref.	Debit	Credit	Balance	
					Debit	Credit

Worksheet for Exercise 4.6

ACCOUNT NAME	TRIAL BALANCE		ADJUSTMENTS		INCOME STATEMENT		BALANCE SHEET	
	DEBIT	CREDIT	DEBIT	CREDIT	DEBIT	CREDIT	DEBIT	CREDIT

JOURNAL								Page	
Date	Account Title and Explanation	Doc No.	Post. Ref.	General Debit		General Credit	

Post-Closing Trial Balance form for Exercise 4.9

ACCOUNT TITLE	ACCT. NO.	DEBIT		CREDIT	

V. OPTIONAL EXERCISES FOR EXTRA CREDIT

Complete the following activity (171 total points).

The general ledger for **Keri Downs, Attorney**, is provided on the following pages. Only the balances are shown to simulate the end of the monthly fiscal period (ended on December 31 of the current year).

1. **Prepare a trial balance on the worksheet provided, and then complete the worksheet**. Use the following information to make the adjustments to update these accounts:

   Inventory for Office Supplies on Dec. 31 – $915.00

   Value of Prepaid Insurance on Dec. 31 – $2,040.00

2. **Prepare an income statement** (review the correct format from Section I of LIFEPAC 6 if necessary).

3. **Prepare a statement of owner's equity**. No additional investments were made by the owner. (Review the correct format from Section II of LIFEPAC 6 if necessary.)

4. **Prepare a report-format balance sheet** (review the correct format from Section III of LIFEPAC 6 if necessary).

5. **Record and post the adjusting entries**. Use page 3 of a journal.

6. **Record and post the closing entries**.

7. **Prepare a post-closing trial balance**.

Account Title: Cash   Account No. 110

Date 20—		Explanation	Post. Ref.	Debit		Credit		Balance Debit		Balance Credit	
Dec.	31		✔					1550	00		

Account Title: Petty Cash   Account No. 120

Date 20—		Explanation	Post. Ref.	Debit		Credit		Balance Debit		Balance Credit	
Dec.	31		✔					200	00		

Account Title: Office Supplies   Account No. 130

Date 20—		Explanation	Post. Ref.	Debit		Credit		Balance Debit		Balance Credit	
Dec.	31		✔					1280	00		

Account Title: Prepaid Insurance   Account No. 140

Date 20—		Explanation	Post. Ref.	Debit		Credit		Balance Debit		Balance Credit	
Dec.	31		✔					2400	00		

Account Title: Law Library   Account No. 150

Date 20—		Explanation	Post. Ref.	Debit		Credit		Balance Debit		Balance Credit	
Dec.	31		✔					2500	00		

Account Title: Equipment   Account No. 160

Date 20—		Explanation	Post. Ref.	Debit		Credit		Balance Debit		Credit	
Dec.	31		✔					5600	00		

Account Title: Computer Services   Account No. 210

Date 20—		Explanation	Post. Ref.	Debit		Credit		Balance Debit		Credit	
Dec.	31		✔							760	00

Account Title: Fox's Office Supply   Account No. 220

Date 20—		Explanation	Post. Ref.	Debit		Credit		Balance Debit		Credit	
Dec.	31		✔							415	00

Account Title: Prentice-Hall   Account No. 230

Date 20—		Explanation	Post. Ref.	Debit		Credit		Balance Debit		Credit	
Dec.	31		✔							1840	00

Account Title: Keri Downs, Capital   Account No. 310

Date 20—		Explanation	Post. Ref.	Debit		Credit		Balance Debit		Credit	
Dec.	31		✔							9200	00

Account Title: Keri Downs, Drawing   **Account No.** 320

Date 20—		Explanation	Post. Ref.	Debit		Credit		Balance			
								Debit		Credit	
Dec.	31		✔					1100	00		

Account Title: Income Summary   **Account No.** 330

Date 20—		Explanation	Post. Ref.	Debit		Credit		Balance			
								Debit		Credit	

Account Title: Legal Fees Income   **Account No.** 410

Date 20—		Explanation	Post. Ref.	Debit		Credit		Balance			
								Debit		Credit	
Dec.	31		✔							5250	00

Account Title: Advertising Expense   **Account No.** 510

Date 20—		Explanation	Post. Ref.	Debit		Credit		Balance			
								Debit		Credit	
Dec.	31		✔					125	00		

Account Title: Insurance Expense   **Account No.** 520

Date 20—		Explanation	Post. Ref.	Debit		Credit		Balance			
								Debit		Credit	

Account Title: Miscellaneous Expense   Account No. 530

Date 20—		Explanation	Post. Ref.	Debit		Credit		Balance Debit		Balance Credit	
Dec.	31		✔					80	00		

Account Title: Rent Expense   Account No. 540

Date 20—		Explanation	Post. Ref.	Debit		Credit		Balance Debit		Balance Credit	
Dec.	1		✔					1000	00		

Account Title: Salary Expense   Account No. 550

Date 20—		Explanation	Post. Ref.	Debit		Credit		Balance Debit		Balance Credit	
Dec.	31		✔					1400	00		

Account Title: Supplies Expense – Office   Account No. 560

Date 20—		Explanation	Post. Ref.	Debit		Credit		Balance Debit		Balance Credit	

Account Title: Utilities Expense   Account No. 570

Date 20—		Explanation	Post. Ref.	Debit		Credit		Balance Debit		Balance Credit	
Dec.	1		✔					230	00		

Worksheet

ACCOUNT NAME	TRIAL BALANCE		ADJUSTMENTS		INCOME STATEMENT		BALANCE SHEET	
	DEBIT	CREDIT	DEBIT	CREDIT	DEBIT	CREDIT	DEBIT	CREDIT

Income Statement:

Statement of Owner's Equity:

Balance Sheet:

Journal:

		JOURNAL							Page
Date	Account Title and Explanation	Doc No.	Post. Ref.	General Debit			General Credit		

Post-Closing Trial Balance:

ACCOUNT TITLE	ACCT. NO.	DEBIT	CREDIT

Worksheet

ACCOUNT NAME	TRIAL BALANCE		ADJUSTMENTS		INCOME STATEMENT		BALANCE SHEET	
	DEBIT	CREDIT	DEBIT	CREDIT	DEBIT	CREDIT	DEBIT	CREDIT

Income Statement:

Statement of Owner's Equity:

Balance Sheet:

Journal:

JOURNAL								Page	
Date		Account Title and Explanation	Doc No.	Post. Ref.	General Debit		General Credit	

Post-Closing Trial Balance:

ACCOUNT TITLE	ACCT. NO.	DEBIT	CREDIT